RECLAIM YOUR SANCTUARY

13 Body-Based Practices for Nervous

System Healing

By

Erlange Elisme, DSW
Elisme Consulting Services LLC

2025

RECLAIM YOUR SANCTUARY

13 Body-Based Practices for Nervous System Healing

ISBN: 978-1-966342-21-2
Printed in the United States of America
First Edition, 2025

TABLE OF CONTENTS

A NOTE FROM THE AUTHOR

For more than thirty years, I have sat with people in their deepest pain. As a bilingual social worker and team leader in Broward County, and later as a school social worker and Foster Care Liaison in Gwinnett County Public Schools, I witnessed what happens when trauma lives in the body without language, without acknowledgment, and without a path toward healing.

I watched children who could not sit still because their nervous systems were overwhelmed. I listened to mothers carrying the weight of their own histories while trying to protect their children from similar wounds. I held space for families displaced by violence, by systems that did not see them, and by circumstances beyond their control.

Working at the intersection of child welfare, education, and family preservation taught me that healing cannot happen in isolation. It requires cultural wisdom, systemic awareness, and a commitment to seeing the humanity in every person.

That work changed me. It taught me that healing is not about thinking our way out of trauma. It is about bringing the body back into safety. It is about teaching the nervous system, through gentle and repeated experience, that this moment—right now—is survivable. That rest is allowed. That care is deserved.

I pursued my doctorate in social work and advanced training in trauma-informed care, global and immigrant mental health, motivational interviewing, and work with survivors of human trafficking to bridge research and real life. But none of that matters without something deeper: the understanding that healing begins with permission. Permission to feel. Permission to rest. Permission to take back what was taken.

These thirteen practices emerged from years of work with diverse communities, from my own healing journey, from cultural wisdom, and from evidence-based neuroscience. They are not meant to replace therapy or professional care. They are meant to be a companion—a gentle way of reclaiming your body as your own.

This book is an offering. My hope is that these practices support you in reclaiming your sanctuary and remind your nervous system that safety is possible.

You are worthy of this. Simply because you are human. Because your body matters.

With deep respect,
Erlange Elisme, DSW
Founder and CEO, Elisme Consulting Services LLC

A NOTE BEFORE YOU BEGIN

This book is not a program. It is not meant to be completed in order. It is not asking anything of you.

These practices are invitations. You may move through them slowly, skip around, or return to the same one again and again. Your body leads here.

If at any point a practice feels overwhelming or uncomfortable, you are allowed to stop. You are allowed to pause. You are allowed to choose something else. Nothing in this book requires pushing through.

This space is meant to support you, not change you.

HOW TO USE THIS BOOK

You can open this book anywhere.

Some days, reading may be enough. Some days, noticing one sensation may be enough. Some days, simply holding the book may be enough.

Each practice includes a visual moment, a body-based invitation, an explanation of how the practice supports the nervous system, practice variations, and a reflection for integration.

You do not need to complete the reflections. You do not need to feel different afterward. Let this book meet you where you are.

THE SCIENCE BEHIND THESE PRACTICES

The practices in this book are grounded in neuroscience and evidence-based research. When stress is present, the body often remains on alert. These responses are adaptive, yet when they persist, they can make it difficult to feel settled.

Body-based practices support regulation by working with the nervous system rather than against it. Gentle awareness of breath, sensation, and movement helps the brain receive updated information about safety in the present moment.

Practices that involve noticing internal sensations support interoception, the brain's ability to sense what is happening inside the body. Sensory grounding practices help orient attention to the here and now, reducing overwhelm.

These practices do not require forcing calm or changing thoughts. Simply observing experience with steadiness can reduce stress, increase flexibility, and support resilience over time.

PRACTICE ONE

The Breath

Place one hand on your belly and one on your heart.
Notice the rise.
Notice the fall.
You do not need to change your breath.
You do not need to slow it down or deepen it.
Just notice that it is already here, moving on its own,
carrying you through this moment.
Right now, you are breathing.
That is enough.

WHAT THIS PRACTICE DOES IN THE BODY

Breathing happens automatically, which makes it one of
the safest places to begin when the nervous system feels
overwhelmed. Because no effort is required, the body
does not interpret this practice as another task to perform.
It is an invitation to notice something that is already
occurring.

Under stress, breathing often becomes shallow or tight.
This is not something to correct. It is a protective
response shaped by the nervous system's need to prepare
for danger. Simply noticing the breath provides updated
information: in this moment, there is no immediate threat
requiring action. The body can resource itself differently.

Placing one hand on the belly and one on the heart adds
sensation. Sensation is how the nervous system learns
safety. This gentle contact can support grounding and

2

containment even if the breath itself does not change. The hands become a way of reassuring the body that it is here, held, and attended to.

This practice does not aim to calm the body. It helps the body orient to the present. Over time, repeated moments of non-effortful awareness can support regulation through familiarity rather than control. The nervous system learns that presence is always available.

PRACTICE VARIATIONS

If the main practice doesn't resonate, you might try:

- Both hands resting on your thighs, simply noticing the breath without touching the body
- One hand placed wherever feels safe, perhaps on an arm or your leg
- Hands in your lap, directing attention to the rhythm of your breath without touch
- Attending to the sensation of breath at the nostrils or in the back of the throat

REFLECTION AND INTEGRATION

Pause for a moment. What did you notice as you followed the breath?

_____

_____

_____

Did anything shift, even slightly?

_____

_____

_____

What was it like to let the breath be exactly as it was?

_____

_____

_____

You can return to this practice anytime. Breathing does not need to be earned. It is already yours.

PRACTICE TWO

The Audible Sigh

Inhale gently through the nose.
Allow the exhale to leave through the mouth as a soft sigh.
There is no need to push.
No need to make it loud.
Notice the pause that follows.
The space.
The settling.
This is not about releasing everything.
It is about allowing a little room.

WHAT THIS PRACTICE DOES IN THE BODY

Exhalation plays a significant role in nervous system regulation. Longer or fuller exhales help signal that immediate action is not required. The nervous system responds to the rhythm of breathing as a signal of safety. When sound is added, vibration travels through the chest, throat, and jaw, areas where tension often accumulates without our noticing.

This practice supports gentle discharge. Rather than holding energy in or forcing it out, the body completes a natural cycle. The nervous system recognizes completion instead of interruption. There is a sense of resolution, even if small.

For many people, stress is held silently. The audible sigh gives the body permission to release without explanation or justification. Over time, this can reduce baseline tension and support emotional flexibility. The body learns that it is safe to be heard.

PRACTICE VARIATIONS

If the main practice doesn't resonate, you might try:

- A silent exhale through the mouth, simply feeling the release without sound
- A gentle hum as you exhale, which still creates vibration but feels more contained
- A long exhale through the nose instead of the mouth, directing release inward
- Simply extending your exhales longer than your inhales, without adding sigh or sound

REFLECTION AND INTEGRATION

What did you notice after the sigh?

_____

_____

_____

Did the pause feel noticeable or subtle?

_____

_____

_____

Sometimes relief begins with permission.

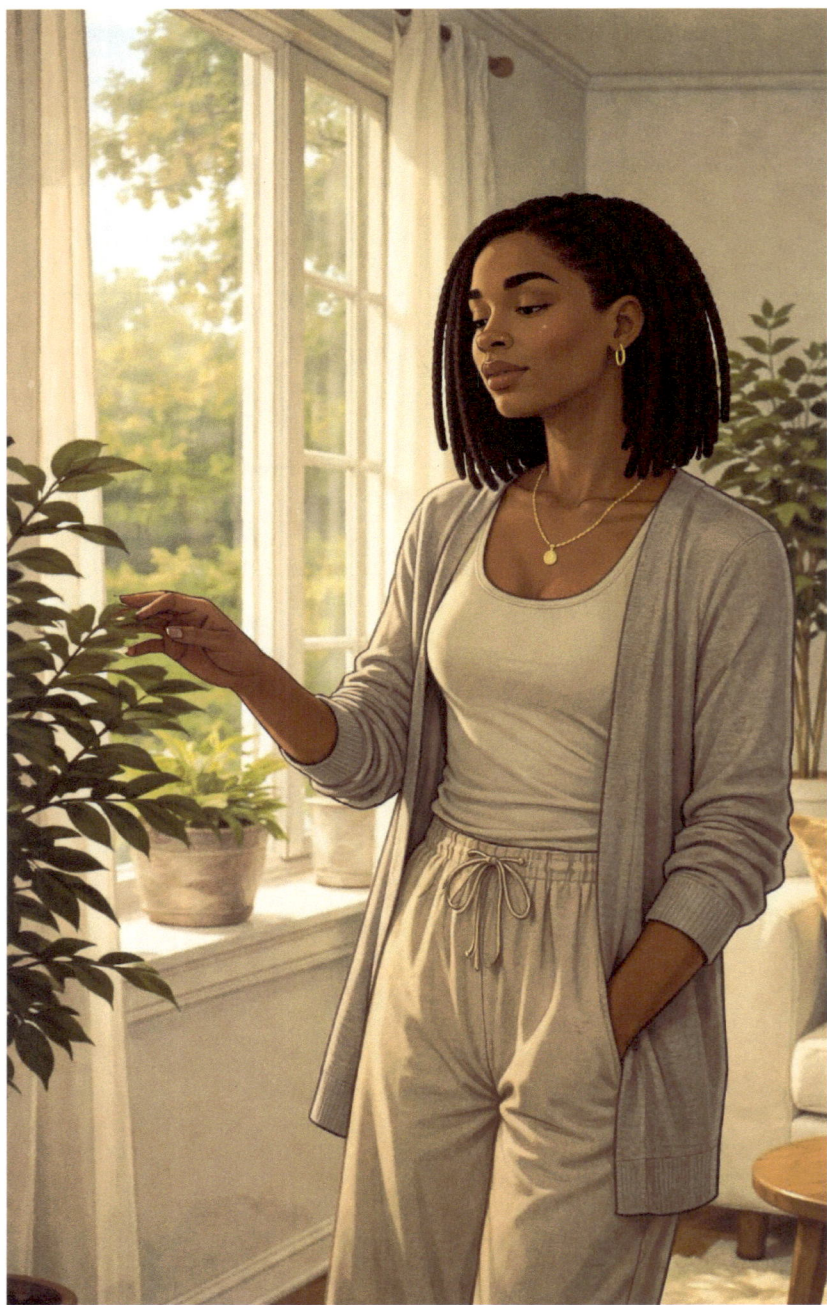

PRACTICE THREE

Five-Senses Grounding

Name five things you can see.
Four things you can feel.
Three things you can hear.
Two things you can smell.
One thing you can taste or sense in your mouth.
Move slowly.
You are helping your body arrive.

WHAT THIS PRACTICE DOES IN THE BODY

When stress or overwhelm is present, attention often pulls away from the present moment. The nervous system may orient toward past experiences or future worries. Sensory grounding gently brings attention back to what is happening now, to the concrete world around you.

Engaging the senses gives the brain clear, concrete information about safety and location. This helps reduce overwhelm by organizing attention around something simple and observable. The body learns where it is and what is happening without needing to analyze or interpret.

This practice does not eliminate distress. It restores orientation. With repetition, sensory grounding can support steadier attention and emotional regulation. The nervous system begins to recognize: I am here. This is where I am. This is what is present.

PRACTICE VARIATIONS

If the main practice doesn't resonate, you might try:

- Three-Two-One: Simply notice three things you see, two you hear, one you feel
- One sense at a time: Spend a full minute noticing only what you see, then what you hear, then what you feel
- Slow walking: Move through your space slowly, deliberately noticing one sense at a time
- Favorite sense focus: Return repeatedly to whichever sense feels most calming to you

REFLECTION AND INTEGRATION

Which sense felt easiest to notice?

_____

_____

_____

What changed as you oriented to your surroundings?

_____

_____

_____

Presence often begins outside the mind.

PRACTICE FOUR

Rooting Like the Great Oak

Bring attention to your feet.
Notice where they meet the ground.
Feel the weight of your body being held.
You do not need to feel strong.
You are allowing support.

WHAT THIS PRACTICE DOES IN THE BODY

Grounding through the feet provides sensory input related to balance, pressure, and stability. These sensations help the nervous system feel supported rather than suspended. When we are caught in stress or anxiety, the body often pulls upward, bracing against threat. Attention rises to the head, the chest tightens, and we lose connection to the ground beneath us.

This practice invites a gentle descent. As you notice the contact between your feet and the earth, the nervous system receives information: I am held. I am supported. I do not have to hold myself up alone. This creates a felt sense of stability that does not depend on forcing strength, but rather on receiving the support that is always available.

The metaphor of the oak is intentional. Great trees do not root themselves through effort. They simply extend themselves into the earth and discover what holds them. You can do the same.

PRACTICE VARIATIONS

If the main practice doesn't resonate, you might try:

- Rooting while seated: Bring attention to where your seat meets the chair, feeling the support beneath you
- Hands to earth: If seated, place your hands on your legs or on the floor to feel connection
- Lying down: Even lying in bed, you can notice the points where your body meets the mattress, feeling held and supported
- Foot pressing: Press your feet firmly into the ground for a few seconds, then release, noticing the rebound

REFLECTION AND INTEGRATION

What did you notice in your body as you brought attention to your feet?

_____

_____

_____

Did anything change in your posture or your sense of presence?

_____

_____

_____

Stability is not the absence of difficulty. It is the experience of being held even when difficulty is present.

PRACTICE FIVE

The Gentle Hand

Place one hand gently on a part of your body that wants
support.
Your heart.
Your belly.
Your arm.
Feel the warmth of your own hand.
Notice the pressure.
Notice the care.
This touch is not forcing anything.
It is witnessing.
It is acknowledging: I am here. I can feel you. You are not
alone.

WHAT THIS PRACTICE DOES IN THE BODY

Touch is one of the most direct pathways to nervous
system regulation. It activates the parasympathetic
nervous system, the part of us that knows how to rest and
recover. When we touch ourselves with gentleness, we are
teaching the body that it is safe to be vulnerable.

The pressure and warmth of a hand communicate care
without words. The nervous system does not distinguish
between being touched by another person and being
touched by yourself. Both can activate the vagus nerve

and create conditions for regulation. Both can send the message: You matter. You deserve this.

This practice is especially powerful for those who have experienced relational harm. It reclaims touch as something that belongs to you. It teaches you that you can be a source of care for yourself.

PRACTICE VARIATIONS

If the main practice doesn't resonate, you might try:

- Hold your own hand gently, as you would a child's hand
- Cross your arms gently across your chest, hands resting on opposite shoulders
- Wrap your arms around yourself in a self-embrace
- Simply rest your hands in your lap, offering them presence and attention

REFLECTION AND INTEGRATION

What did you feel when your hand made contact?

_____

_____

_____

Was it easy or did it feel strange?

_____

_____

_____

Either response is welcome. Healing sometimes begins with the strange becoming familiar.

PRACTICE SIX

Body Scan with Compassion

Without judgment, notice what sensations are present in
your body.
Warmth.
Coolness.
Tightness.
Ease.
Whatever is here.
You are not trying to change anything.
You are simply looking, as you might look at a landscape.
With curiosity.
With tenderness.
Whatever you find is allowed to be there.

WHAT THIS PRACTICE DOES IN THE BODY

Many of us have learned to disconnect from our bodies.
We override signals of fatigue, discomfort, and need
because we were taught that our bodies are not
trustworthy, or that attending to them is selfish. A body
scan begins the slow work of reconnection.

This practice strengthens interoception, our ability to
sense what is happening inside ourselves. As interoceptive
awareness grows, we gain access to information we may
have been ignoring. We learn what our body needs. We

develop the capacity to name and address discomfort before it becomes overwhelming.

The emphasis on compassion is crucial. Many practices ask us to observe without judgment. But this practice asks us to observe with care. To notice our body not as a problem to fix, but as part of ourselves that deserves attention and kindness. This shifts the entire nervous system response from correction toward acceptance.

PRACTICE VARIATIONS

If the main practice doesn't resonate, you might try:

- **Partial scan:** Focus on just the upper body, or just below the waist
- **Single point:** Spend several minutes noticing sensation in just your hands or feet
- **Guided:** Listen to a recorded body scan to help guide your attention
- **Movement-based:** Notice sensations as you slowly move through gentle stretches

REFLECTION AND INTEGRATION

What did you notice?

_____

_____

_____

Where did you feel most present?

_____

_____

_____

Was there a part of your body that felt separate from your awareness?

_____

_____

_____

These are not problems to solve. They are simply information about where your attention naturally goes, and where you might offer more gentle presence over time.

PRACTICE SEVEN
Thoughts Like Clouds

Notice the thoughts that move through your mind.
Rather than following them, imagine them like clouds
passing through the sky.
They come.
They drift.
They dissolve.
You do not need to push them away. You do not need
to hold them. They are simply passing through.

WHAT THIS PRACTICE DOES IN THE BODY

Thoughts often feel urgent when the nervous system is
activated. Especially thoughts about threat, failure, or
danger. When we merge with these thoughts, believing
them to be truth, the nervous system continues to
respond as though the danger is real and immediate.
Observing thoughts rather than merging with them
creates distance and reduces reactivity.

This practice engages parts of the brain associated with
awareness and perspective. The prefrontal cortex, which
helps us think about thinking, becomes more active. The
body learns that thoughts can move without requiring
action or belief. A thought that says "I am worthless" can

be noticed and allowed to pass, just like a cloud. This does not mean ignoring the thought. It means recognizing that thoughts arise from the nervous system's attempt to protect us, not from truth about who we are.

Over time, this supports cognitive flexibility and reduces mental overload. The mind becomes a sky, and thoughts become weather. Both are welcome.

PRACTICE VARIATIONS

If the main practice doesn't resonate, you might try:

- River thoughts: Imagine thoughts like leaves floating down a river, moving away from you
- Distance: Notice thoughts as if they are happening on a distant horizon
- Label and release: Simply say "thinking" as you notice a thought, then return attention to breath
- Write it down: Externalize the thought by writing it on paper, then set it aside

REFLECTION AND INTEGRATION

What changed when you allowed thoughts to pass?

_____

_____

_____

Did the ones you were watching dissolve, or did they linger?

_____

_____

_____

Relief often comes from space, from the recognition that we are not our thoughts. We are the sky in which they move.

PRACTICE EIGHT

Naming the Cloud

Notice what feels most present.
A sensation.
An emotion.
A thought.
Offer it one simple word.
Tightness.
Sadness.
Worry.
Pause.

WHAT THIS PRACTICE DOES IN THE BODY

The brain processes language and sensation differently. Raw sensation without language can feel chaotic or overwhelming. Naming sensations and emotions helps organize experience. Language provides structure, allowing the nervous system to move from raw sensation toward regulation.

When we cannot name what we are feeling, we remain identified with it. The feeling becomes our entire world. When we can name it, we create some distance. We say, "I am experiencing sadness" rather than "I am sad." This small shift in language creates a small shift in our relationship to the experience.

This practice reduces overwhelm by clarifying what is present without analysis. It does not ask us to fix or change anything. Just to name. The body learns that experience can be named without being consumed by it. Clarity can begin with one word.

PRACTICE VARIATIONS

If the main practice doesn't resonate, you might try:

- Short phrase: Use two or three words ("sharp pain," "heavy sadness")
- Color or texture: Name the feeling by color or texture ("blue-gray," "sandpaper feeling")
- Imagery: Describe what the feeling reminds you of ("like waves," "like a storm")
- No words: Simply nod or gesture acknowledgment of what is present

REFLECTION AND INTEGRATION

Did naming change anything?

_____

_____

_____

Did the sensation shift, become softer, or did it simply feel more known?

_____

_____

_____

Both are valuable outcomes. Sometimes the point is not transformation, but recognition.

PRACTICE NINE

Loving-Kindness for the Self

Offer yourself simple phrases of care, only if they feel accessible. There is no need to feel them fully.
May I be gentle with myself.
May I know I am worthy.
May I feel the support of this moment.
Or simply repeat a word or phrase that speaks to you.
Peace. Ease. I am here.

WHAT THIS PRACTICE DOES IN THE BODY

Supportive language can activate systems related to care and connection. These systems help balance threat responses and self-criticism. When the nervous system is dysregulated, it defaults to a protective stance. We become harsh with ourselves, viewing our struggles as failures rather than human experiences. Loving-kindness practices gently shift us toward self-compassion.

For many people, self-kindness feels unfamiliar or undeserved. The practices that emerge from trauma histories often teach us that we must earn care through achievement or perfection. This practice respects that history by allowing neutrality or distance. You do not need to feel loving-kindness deeply. Offering the phrases, allowing them to be present, is enough. Healing moves slowly, and sometimes the first step is simply not being cruel to ourselves.

Over time, gentle self-directed care can support emotional buffering and resilience. The nervous system learns that there is an ally within, and that ally is you.

PRACTICE VARIATIONS

If the main practice doesn't resonate, you might try:

- Statement of fact: "I am doing my best" or "I am trying"
- Gentle directive: "Be kind to yourself" or "You deserve rest"
- Compassion for a friend: Offer to yourself the words you would say to someone you love
- Simply breathe: Release words altogether and rest in gentle presence with yourself

REFLECTION AND INTEGRATION

Which phrase felt possible?

_____

_____

_____

Did offering kindness to yourself feel natural or did it feel forced?

_____

_____

_____

Either response is welcome. Care can begin as an offering, even when it does not yet feel like home.

PRACTICE TEN

The Inner Light

Imagine or sense a steady presence within you.
A light.
A warmth.
A knowing.
There is nothing to create.
It is already there.
Simply notice it.
This is the part of you that witnesses.
That continues.
That remains.

WHAT THIS PRACTICE DOES IN THE BODY

Imagery is powerful. The brain responds to imagined environments and beings in ways similar to real ones when sensory details are involved. When the nervous system is in survival mode, everything feels temporary and unstable. We lose access to a felt sense of continuity. This practice offers that stability through imagery.

The inner light represents the part of us that is not subject to our circumstances. Not the ego, which clings to outcomes, but the awareness that observes both pain and joy without being defined by either. When we connect with this steadiness, the nervous system finds an anchor point. Attention rests on something constant rather than shifting demands.

This practice supports internal orientation and emotional steadiness, especially during uncertainty. When the world feels chaotic, we can return to the recognition that something within us is stable. Something within us has witnessed every challenge we have survived, and it knows we can navigate this moment too.

PRACTICE VARIATIONS

If the main practice doesn't resonate, you might try:

- Solid presence: A stone or anchor within you that is unmovable
- Living presence: A tree, river, or heartbeat that persists
- Spaciousness: A vast internal space that can hold everything
- Witnessing quality: Simply the knowing part of you, without form

REFLECTION AND INTEGRATION

What felt constant?

_____

_____

_____

Was the light always there or did you have to search for it?

_____

_____

_____

Did it feel warm or cool, bright or soft?

_____

_____

_____

Steadiness often remains quietly, available when we need it. You do not have to feel it to access it.

PRACTICE ELEVEN

The Safe Haven

Imagine a place of rest. It can be a place you know or
have known. It can be something that emerges from
your imagination.
A room.
A garden.
A cabin.
The shore.
Enter only as much as feels safe.
You might smell something.
Hear something.
Feel the temperature of the air. Allow yourself to rest
here, if only for this moment.

WHAT THIS PRACTICE DOES IN THE BODY

Safety imagery can support containment and recovery.
When the nervous system has learned to associate certain
environments with threat, real or imagined, it remains
hypervigilant. Safety imagery gradually teaches the
nervous system that some spaces, some moments, are
indeed secure.

The sensory details matter enormously. The more specific
the imagery, the more potent the effect. If you can smell
the earth after rain or hear the soft call of birds, the brain's

sensory cortex becomes engaged. The entire nervous system participates in the feeling of safety.

Choice is central. The body decides how close is enough. Do not push yourself deeper into the image if it does not feel right. Some days you might see your safe haven clearly. Other days it might be hazy. Both are acceptable. What matters is that you are teaching your nervous system that safety, and rest, are accessible to you.

PRACTICE VARIATIONS

If the main practice doesn't resonate, you might try:

- Use a real place: Return mentally to a place where you actually felt safe
- Remember the feeling: Focus on the sensation of safety rather than the visual image
- Combine with anchor: Hold an object or person while imagining a safe place
- Single element: Imagine just one detail (a comfortable chair, soft light) rather than a whole place.

REFLECTION AND INTEGRATION

What qualities felt supportive in your safe haven?

_____

_____

_____

Was there something living there, or was it a quiet space?

_____

_____

_____

Safety begins with permission. Permission to rest, to be held by something larger than our struggles, to belong to a space that is ours.

PRACTICE TWELVE
Gratitude for the Small

Notice one small, ordinary moment of ease.
A sip of something warm. Sunlight on your skin.
A moment where nothing hurt. Let it be enough.

WHAT THIS PRACTICE DOES IN THE BODY

The nervous system is naturally attuned to threat. It is shaped by evolution to notice danger, to protect us from harm. This adaptation saved our ancestors many times over. But in a world where the perceived threats never fully resolve, where stress becomes chronic, this protective mechanism begins to work against us. We miss the moments of ease because we are looking for danger.

Noticing small moments of ease widens attention and reduces vigilance. It does not minimize pain. It does not dismiss struggle. It simply balances awareness. It says: Yes, hard things are present. And look, this moment is okay. This breath is okay. This warmth is okay.

Over time, as we practice noticing moments of ease, our set point shifts. We become slightly less vigilant. The nervous system begins to recognize that safety is possible, even if it was not safe before. Gratitude in this sense is not toxic positivity. It is a nervous system strategy that allows us to experience the full spectrum of life, not just its dangers.

PRACTICE VARIATIONS

If the main practice doesn't resonate, you might try:

- Notice without gratitude: Simply observe moments of ease without labeling them as good
- Neutral attention: "This happened" instead of "I am grateful for this"
- Relief: Notice moments that were less painful rather than actively good
- Acknowledgment: Simply recognize "I survived this moment" without adding more

REFLECTION AND INTEGRATION

What did you notice?

_____

_____

_____

Was it easy to find a moment of ease, or did you have to search?

_____

_____

_____

Steadiness grows in small moments. The nervous system learns to recognize safety not as the absence of difficulty, but as the presence of moments we can rest in.

PRACTICE THIRTEEN
The Final Affirmation

Offer yourself a simple, present-focused affirmation.
One that speaks to where you are right now.
I am breathing.
I am here.
This moment will pass.
I can find my way through.
Let it land where it can.

WHAT THIS PRACTICE DOES IN THE BODY

Grounded affirmations help orient the nervous system in time. They remind the body that moments move and change. When we are trapped in dysregulation, time collapses. One painful moment becomes forever. An affirmation that reminds us "this moment will pass" or "I can find my way through" restores our relationship to time and to our own capacity.

This practice supports integration rather than resolution. It does not promise that everything will become easy or that the struggle will end. It simply reminds us that we have moved through difficult moments before. That we have resources, even if we cannot feel them in this moment. That presence is available, even when comfort is not.

The nervous system internalizes these truths gradually, through repetition and lived experience. Each time you return to this affirmation, you are teaching yourself something essential: I am still here. I am still moving. I am still worthy of care.

PRACTICE VARIATIONS

If the main practice doesn't resonate, you might try:

- Micro affirmation: "I am trying" or "I showed up"
- Question instead: "What do I need right now?" rather than a statement
- Body-based: "My heart is beating. I am alive." or "My body is here."
- Borrowed words: Use lyrics, poetry, or quotes from someone you trust.

REFLECTION AND INTEGRATION

What felt true enough?

_____

_____

_____

Did the affirmation shift something, or did it simply sit with you?

_____

_____

_____

Presence is enough. Presence does not require transformation. It requires only that we show up, again and again, for ourselves and for this moment.

WHEN PRACTICES FEEL DIFFICULT

If you find yourself struggling with a practice, you are not doing anything wrong. Some practices will resonate immediately. Others will take time. Some may never feel right for you, and that is completely acceptable.

What to Do If a Practice Feels Overwhelming
If you notice strong emotion, flashback, or physical distress:

- Stop immediately. There is no prize for pushing through.
- Ground yourself: Open your eyes wide. Feel your feet. Name objects around you.
- Move your body: Stand up, shake out hands, splash cool water.
- Skip this practice. Return to one that feels safer.
- If reactions persist, reach out to a trauma-informed mental health professional.

What to Do If a Practice Feels Ineffective
If you try a practice and nothing happens, you have not failed.

- Try the practice variation. Small adjustments help.
- Return another day. Your nervous system may be ready then.

- Combine it with another practice that feels more natural.
- Give yourself permission to skip it. Not every practice is for every person.

What to Do If You Feel Nothing

For many who have experienced significant stress or trauma, the ability to feel sensation becomes difficult. This is not failure. It is protection.

- Start smaller. Notice one breath instead of many.
- Engage sensation from outside: cold water, warm drink, pressure.
- Return to grounding practices repeatedly. Awareness develops with time.
- Consider working with a trauma-informed somatic therapist.

BUILDING A PERSONAL PRACTICE

After working with individual practices, you may want to weave them together into something more sustained.

Practice Sequences for Different Needs

For acute overwhelm:

- Rooting Like the Great Oak (5 min) - ground physically
- Five-Senses Grounding (3 min) - orient to environment
- The Breath (2 min) - signal safety

For low-level anxiety:

- The Breath (5 min) - arrive in body
- Body Scan with Compassion (7 min) - develop awareness
- Gratitude for the Small (3 min) - shift toward resources

For shame and self-criticism:

- The Gentle Hand (5 min) - activate compassion
- Loving-Kindness for the Self (7 min) - deepen care
- The Final Affirmation (3 min) - integrate and anchor

Creating a Daily Practice

For sustainable daily practice:

- Choose a realistic time (morning, lunch, evening) - commit to 10-15 minutes
- Select 2-3 practices that resonate, not all thirteen
- Rotate through them: one grounding, one awareness, one integration
- Let the practice evolve as your needs change
- On difficult days, 2-3 minutes is enough

PRACTICES IN CONTEXT: REAL-WORLD EXAMPLES

Sometimes it helps to see how practices show up in actual moments. These are composite examples reflecting patterns many people recognize.

Scenario One: The Unexpected Trigger

You are at work when someone raises their voice. Your chest tightens. You feel yourself going back to when you were not safe. Your body does not know the difference between then and now.

Instead of pushing through, you excuse yourself. You plant your feet on the floor. You count five things you can see. Your body begins to receive updated information: I am here. It is 2025. I am in a safe place.

By the time you return, you are not healed, but you are present. You have taught your nervous system that you can resourcefully move through a trigger.

Scenario Two: The Difficult Conversation

You have been avoiding a conversation. Your body is braced. You know you need to talk, but you feel paralyzed.

Before the conversation, you spend five minutes with The Gentle Hand. You place your hand on your heart and remind yourself: I can do hard things. You offer yourself

The Audible Sigh, giving your body permission to release tension.

You are still nervous, but you are not disconnected from yourself. You remain tethered to your own care.

Scenario Three: The Insomnia Night
It is 3 a.m. Your mind is running. You are frustrated that you are not asleep.

Instead of fighting, you try Thoughts Like Clouds. You notice the worries as weather passing through. You do not judge the thoughts. You simply observe them.

You may not fall asleep immediately. But your body begins to relax because you have stopped fighting it. Sometimes rest comes through acceptance.

Scenario Four: The Grief
You have experienced a loss. Someone important is no longer here. Your nervous system knows only that something is missing.

You spend time with Naming the Cloud. Whatever is present (sadness, anger, numbness), you give it one simple word. You do not try to change it. You simply name it, which is a form of witnessing.

These practices do not take away the loss. But they remind you that you can move through loss while still being okay.

RETURNING AGAIN AND AGAIN

You have moved through thirteen practices. But this is not the end. There is no end.

Healing is not linear. Some days these practices will feel like coming home. Other days they will feel distant. This is normal. The nervous system does not move in a straight line. It spirals. It returns. It surprises us.

Return to whichever practice feels right. Return to the Breath when you need grounding. Return to Rooting Like the Great Oak when you need to remember that you are held. Return to Loving-Kindness when you have been too hard on yourself.

As you work with these practices, you are training your nervous system to recognize safety. Not the absence of pain, but the presence of a moment you can move through. Not the elimination of difficulty, but the capacity to rest within it. Not perfection, but presence.

This work is sacred because it is about you. The sanctuary you are reclaiming already exists. It is within you. It has been within you all along.

Trust yourself. Trust your body. Trust the small moments of ease. They are real. They are evidence of your resilience. They are proof that even in difficulty, there is grace.

RESEARCH AND REFERENCES

The practices in this book are grounded in contemporary neuroscience, psychology, and trauma-informed care research. All citations are in APA 7th Edition format.

Foundational Works

Damasio, A. (1999). The feeling of what happens: Body and emotion in the making of consciousness. New York, NY: Harcourt Brace.

Portges, S. W. (2011). The polyvagal theory: Neurophysiological foundations of emotions, attachment, communication, and self-regulation. New York, NY: W. W. Norton & Company.

Siegel, D. J. (2012). The developing mind: How relationships and the brain interact to shape who we are (2nd ed.). New York, NY: Guilford Press.

Breath, Autonomic Nervous System, and Regulation

Noble, D. J., & Hochman, S. (2019). Hypothesis: Pulmonary afferent activity patterns during slow, deep breathing contribute to the neural induction of physiological relaxation. Frontiers in Physiology, 10, 1176. https://doi.org/10.3389/fphys.2019.01176

Russo, M. A., Santarelli, D. M., & O'Rourke, D. (2017). The physiological effects of slow breathing in the healthy human. Breathe, 13(4), 298–309. https://doi.org/10.1183/20734735.009817

Zaccaro, A., Piarulli, A., Laurino, M., Garbella, E., Menicucci, D., Neri, B., & Gemignani, A. (2018). How breath-control can change your life: A systematic review on psychophysiological correlates of slow breathing. Frontiers in Human Neuroscience, 12, 353. https://doi.org/10.3389/fnhum.2018.00353

Sensation, Interoception, and Body Awareness

Farb, N. A. S., Segal, Z. V., & Anderson, A. K. (2013). Mindfulness meditation training alters cortical representations of interoceptive attention. Social Cognitive and Affective Neuroscience, 8(1), 15–26. https://doi.org/10.1093/scan/nsr104

Khalsa, S. S., Adolphs, R., Cameron, O. G., Critchley, H. D., Davenport, P. W., Feinstein, J. S., ... Paulus, M. P. (2018). Interoception and mental health: A roadmap. Biological Psychiatry: Cognitive Neuroscience and Neuroimaging, 3(6), 501–513. https://doi.org/10.1016/j.bpsc.2017.12.004

Price, C. J., & Hooven, C. (2018). Interoceptive awareness skills for emotion regulation: Theory and approach of Mindful Awareness in Body-Oriented Therapy (MABT). Frontiers in Psychology, 9, 798. https://doi.org/10.3389/fpsyg.2018.00798

Safety, Imagery, and Self-Soothing

Brewin, C. R., Gregory, J. D., Lipton, M., & Burgess, N. (2010). Intrusive images in psychological disorders: Characteristics, neural mechanisms, and treatment implications. Psychological Review, 117(1), 210–232. https://doi.org/10.1037/a0018113

Payne, P., Levine, P. A., & Crane-Godreau, M. A. (2015). Somatic experiencing: Using interoception and proprioception as core elements of trauma therapy. Frontiers in Psychology, 6, 93. https://doi.org/10.3389/fpsyg.2015.00093

Mindfulness, Attention, and Cognitive Flexibility

Kabat-Zinn, J. (2003). Mindfulness-based interventions in context: Past, present, and future. Clinical Psychology: Science and Practice, 10(2), 144–156. https://doi.org/10.1093/clipsy.bpg016

Positive Affect and Attentional Balance

Donald, J. N., Bradshaw, E. L., Ryan, R. M., Basarkod, G., Ciarrochi, J., Duineveld, J. J., & Sahdra, B. K. (2020). Mindfulness and its association with varied types of motivation: A systematic review and meta-analysis. Journal of Personality, 88(4), 701–725. https://doi.org/10.1111/jopy.12508

Kok, B. E., & Fredrickson, B. L. (2010). Upward spirals of the heart: Autonomic flexibility, positive emotions, and vagal tone. Psychological Science, 21(11), 1360–1366. https://doi.org/10.1177/0956797610382287

ABOUT THE AUTHOR

Erlange Elisme, DSW, is Founder and CEO of Elisme Consulting Services LLC, a trauma-informed care leadership and consulting firm. She brings over thirty years of experience as a school social worker, including bilingual work with students and families in Broward County, Florida, and as Foster Care Liaison for Gwinnett County Public Schools in Georgia.

Erlange holds advanced certifications from Harvard Medical School in Global Mental Health: Trauma and Recovery, Trauma-Informed Care, Immigrant Mental Health, and Motivational Interviewing. She is also certified in trauma-informed care with survivors of human trafficking. She is fluent in English, French, and Haitian Creole.

Through Elisme Consulting Services, Erlange provides specialized training in trauma-informed leadership and practice, facilitates community and organizational healing initiatives, and develops evidence-based resources for diverse populations. She is the author of multiple books, including Anchored and Unshaken: Restoring the Soul of Haitian Women through Faith, Culture, and Sacred Rest, as well as children's books and mindfulness resources. She hosts the Resilient Voices podcast in both English and Haitian Creole.

Erlange's work integrates cultural wisdom with evidence-based trauma-informed practices, particularly in service of immigrant communities and those affected by displacement, violence, and systemic inequity. She was named a 2025 Gwinnett Chamber Business Excellence Awards finalist in recognition of her contributions to community resilience and healing.

For more information about trainings, consulting services, and resources, visit www.elismeconsultingservices.com or contact elisme@elismeconsultingservices.com

www.ingramcontent.com/pod-product-compliance
Lightning Source LLC
Chambersburg PA
CBHW041522090426
42737CB00037B/13